Little Books on Liturgy

Samuel Torvend, series editor

Also in the series:
For the Life of the World: The Essentials of Episcopal Worship
   by Samuel Torvend
Much Fine Gold: The Revised Common Lectionary
   by Gail Ramshaw

MARCUS GEORGE HALLEY

ABIDE IN PEACE

HEALING AND RECONCILIATION

**A little
book on
liturgy**

CHURCH
PUBLISHING
INCORPORATED

Unless otherwise noted, the Scripture quotations contained herein are from the New Revised Standard Version Bible, copyright © 1989 by the Division of Christian Education of the National Council of Churches of Christ in the United States of America. Used by permission. All rights reserved worldwide.

Church Publishing Incorporated
19 East 34th Street
New York, NY 10016

Cover design by Jennifer Kopec, 2Pug Design
Typeset by Progressive Publishing Services

Library of Congress Cataloging-in-Publication Data
A record of this book is available from the Library of Congress.

ISBN-13: 978-1-64065-420-4 (paperback)
ISBN-13: 978-1-64065-421-1 (ebook)

Contents

Introduction   vii

1 ▪ Creation and Vocation   1

2 ▪ Baptism and the Emergence of Humanity   15

3 ▪ The Reconciliation of a Penitent   27

4 ▪ Ministration to the Sick   39

5 ▪ A World Healed and Reconciled   51

Bibliography   63

Introduction

Blessed are the peacemakers, for they will be called children of God.

—Matt. 5:9

One of the places where I first learned what it meant to be a peacemaker was the Absalom Jones Center in Atlanta, Georgia, where I served as an intern for a year while enrolled at the Interdenominational Theological Center. Before it was the Absalom Jones Center for Racial Healing, the Absalom Jones Episcopal Center was the campus ministry center of the Episcopal Diocese of Atlanta; it served the five historically Black institutions that comprise the Atlanta University Center (AUC): Morris Brown College, Spelman College, Morehouse College, Interdenominational Theological Center, and Clark Atlanta University. Founded with a common mission to educate and empower newly emancipated Black Americans shortly after the conclusion of the US Civil War, the separate institutions of the AUC seemed to possess a common vision of a healed and reconciled world, a vision that has inspired students for more than 150 years.

The AUC is sacred ground, the place that birthed and nurtured the Atlanta Student Movement in the 1960s, the civil rights campaign that featured student sit-ins and demonstrations against Jim Crow segregation. Whether desegregating lunch counters or speaking up for the basic human rights of all people, this campaign cast a vision for healing and reconciliation through struggle. Many leaders of the civil rights movement were either educated in the AUC or had some sort of involvement with it during their work as activists, including Martin Luther King Jr., Coretta Scott King, Julian Bond, and Marian Wright Edelman. The very ground we walked on seemed to call us to a particular vocation: peacemaker.

During my time as the intern, Wednesday celebrations of Eucharist were nothing out of the ordinary. We would gather in the small but neatly appointed chapel at six o'clock in the evening. Only a few of us were students in the AUC. Other members of our community were from the broader community: an older woman who regularly fostered young boys, a young gay couple who were spiritual refugees from an unwelcoming Christian community, and occasionally staff from the surrounding institutions. Each of us was drawn to the Absalom Jones Center for our own reasons. What held us all together was some unseen connection, a desire to be with one another, to worship together, and to spend time in conversation with one another late into the evening, and occasionally into the early morning hours. These conversations seemed to run the gamut from Anglican novices debating what we thought were the finer points of Anglican theology to listening deeply to stories of triumph and trauma, identity and hope.

It was within the walls of the Absalom Jones Center that I learned that the call to be a peacemaker is a call to put one's self in the vulnerable, terrifying place of being in close relationship with others. Simply put: To follow the way of Jesus of Nazareth is to voluntarily place one's self within the imperfect embrace of the community that bears his name as we struggle together, learn to love one another, to forgive one another, to hold and support one another, all the while learning what it truly means to be human.

On one particular Wednesday, something quite apart from the ordinary occurred. The Eucharist was the same, but for whatever reason the words struck me differently. I cannot quite pinpoint what it was exactly. I simply felt called to take the words of the liturgy *seriously*, particularly the words that called me to be a peacemaker. During the Peace, I approached a member of the community I had offended, told him I was wrong, and asked for his forgiveness. He looked surprised at first, but slowly the wall of bitterness he had built using the stones of my arrogance began to collapse. He accepted, we embraced, and the liturgy continued. It was a normal Wednesday-evening Eucharist, but that moment is one that continues to echo in my soul. In that one moment I recognized the power that is present within the Church's vocation of reconciliation. I also experienced the sensation of reconciliation made: incarnate, tangible, and real. I began to recognize that a commitment to peacemaking requires trusting relationships and the embodied experience of putting that relationship back together when we have torn it apart.

Paul the apostle wrote to the church in Corinth that the essence of God's work in the Messiah, Jesus Christ, is one of reconciliation: "So if anyone is in Christ, there is a new creation: everything old has passed away; see, everything has become new! All this is from God, who reconciled us to himself through Christ, and has given us the ministry of reconciliation" (2 Cor. 5:17–18). The word "reconcile" simply means "to bring back together." It is not simply a joining but a *re-joining*. When Christians say that we are a community of reconciliation, we make a bold proclamation to the world that, despite all evidence to the contrary, the normal state of human relationships with God, with one another, with ourselves, and with Creation is one of harmony and justice. The separation that we experience as a result of human sin and brokenness is an aberration of God's intention for us.

Christians also believe that the work of reconciliation is ultimately God's work accomplished in Jesus Christ in which we, God's baptized people, are called to share. The Book of Common Prayer uses the phrase "Paschal Mystery" to speak to this. The Paschal Mystery refers to the inexhaustible well of meaning and significance found in and around the death and the resurrection of Jesus Christ. Jesus and his saving work stand at the heart of the Christian witness. It isn't simply that Jesus teaches us something; Jesus *accomplishes* something revealed in his life and teachings. In the words of the Church of Scotland's baptismal liturgy:

> For you Jesus Christ came into the world:
> for you he lived and showed God's love;
> for you he suffered the darkness of Calvary
> and cried at the last, "It is accomplished";
> for you he triumphed over death and rose in newness of life;
> for you he ascended to reign at God's right hand.
> All this he did for you, little one,
> though you do not know it yet.

God has done something in Jesus that accomplishes the reconciliation the world needed. God has made the world new through the Messiah. Our work is to participate in God's work of reconciliation especially when the world around us seems stuck in division and brokenness. This is one takeaway from Jesus's oft-repeated words: "... The Kingdom of God has come near ..." (Mark 1:15). It is here, incredibly present, and yet not fully here. Our call is to live in the age to come—the reconciled age—in our own present one.

If we are to take Paul's words to the Corinthian church to heart, then we see that the clear vocation of the Church in the world is to be the community of people made new by Christ who proclaim the reality of the Resurrection and then seek to live out the implications of the new life—namely, we become *reconciled reconcilers*. In every space and place where inhumane action and behavior contribute to the suffering of self and others, the exploitation of creation, and the dishonoring of God, the Church is called to the front lines, to heal the broken, and to mend what has been torn apart. God has done the ultimate healing and reconciliation. What is left for us is to draw attention to God's healing presence in the world. We've been healed by the graciousness of God. We are called to heal others. When the world asks Jeremiah's age-old question, "is there no balm in Gilead?" we respond by echoing the words of Africans held in chattel bondage, "There is a Balm in Gilead to make the wounded soul. There is a Balm in Gilead to heal the sin-sick soul."

The need for reconciled reconcilers is especially pronounced in our age. In the United States, we live in a society where the alienation and separation are visible in our communities, our schools, our businesses, and even our houses of worship. Ours is a highly stratified society, one that sorts us by race and ethnicity, socioeconomic class, religion, and political party affiliation. These differences are not merely unfortunate or inconvenient; in many cases, these differences are matters of life and death, especially for those sorted to the bottom of our society.

In the past, mainline churches in the United States often neglected our vocation to be reconciled reconcilers, choosing instead to be keepers and guardians of a harmful status quo. If behavior is an indicator of one's highest ideal, then the highest ideal of the American mainline church has been and continues to be respectability, not reconciliation. We would often rather "keep" the peace than "make" peace. Martin Luther King Jr. said as much in his "Letter from a Birmingham Jail," where he chides "the white moderate" who prefers a "a negative peace which is the absence of tension" rather than "a positive peace which is the presence of justice." Toward the end of his iconic letter, King said, "If today's church does not recapture the sacrificial spirit of the early church, it will lose its authenticity, forfeit the loyalty of millions, and be dismissed as an irrelevant social club with no meaning for the twentieth century."

In saying this, Dr. King channeled the message of Paul the apostle. Our purpose is reconciliation, and if we are not committed to that work, we may as well close up shop. The Atlanta Student Movement of the 1960s and the Black Lives Matter movement of our time hold up the uncomfortable truth which we must either accept or turn away: The peace we seek can only come through confrontation and struggle. We must shake off respectability, shake up the status quo, and put on the vocation of reconciliation and healing if we are to truly be the church.

Ours is a ministry of reconciliation. The church is most truly and authentically the church when we are on the front lines of human suffering and pain, embodying the work of Jesus, mending the broken, caring for the suffering, giving of ourselves so that others may live. What follows is an exploration of reconciliation through the intersection of Holy Scriptures and our liturgical practice. What I write here is a reflection on the liturgical rites for reconciliation and healing from the prayer book—the rites for the "Reconciliation of a Penitent" and "Ministration to the Sick," respectively—but also to explore the wider theological territory of reconciliation and healing. My goal is to help each reader reflect not simply on how we experience reconciliation and healing personally, but how we connect that personal experience to God's cosmic work of reconciliation to the world in which we live. My guiding liturgical principle is this: Liturgy is only Christian liturgy when those who engage in it do so with the understanding that we are participating in God's liturgy—the healing and reconciliation of the world already accomplished in Jesus. Liturgy is not the work of the people alone. Christian liturgy is our work with God that imagines and participates in God's new creation.

We will begin our journey in the first chapter by exploring the significance of the Creation stories in Genesis and what they say about the uniqueness of the human vocation along with how this understanding helps us to diagnose the problem at the heart of the human condition, namely sin. In chapter two, we will listen to what our liturgical practice suggests about the human condition and our need for redemption by examining the two sacraments that form the basis for the Christian identity and vocation and thus inform every other sacrament: baptism and Eucharist. Chapter three focuses our attention on the rite for the "Reconciliation of a Penitent," particularly how we experience and appropriate this rite and the grace it communicates. Chapter four considers the "Ministration to the Sick." Chapter five builds on each of the previous chapters and seeks to cast a compelling vision for the kingdom of God, the end toward which the Church both journeys and points and the present and future reality our sacramental tradition assumes. In each chapter, we will reflect on the contemporary and contextual implications of each subject and attempt to draw out tangible and tactile responses to the need for reconciliation in our own world.

As I experienced many years ago at the Absalom Jones Center, so much becomes possible when we take our rites and rituals seriously, when we bring them close and allow them to reshape our minds and our muscles, thereby making peacemaking second nature. It is no accident for me that Absalom Jones Center is named for a man who spent his life as a peacemaker, working to build bridges between white and Black Episcopalians when so many white Episcopalians treated him as less than human even at great risk to himself. His name literally means "father of peace."

He was a peacemaker, and the center that bears his name taught me about peace. I hope to be able to offer some reflection to share that wisdom with others.

Reflection Questions

1. When you think of "peace," what images come to mind? What sources or influences inform your understanding of peace?

2. The Book of Common Prayer (833) contains "A Prayer Attributed to St. Francis," that asks God to "make us instruments of [God's] peace." How do you see this prayer as part of your faith? Where does this prayer challenge your understanding of what it means to follow Jesus?

3. Consider the definition of worship offered here: "Liturgy is not the work of the people alone. Christian liturgy is our work with God that imagines and participates in God's new creation." What does this understanding of worship, of liturgy, bring to mind? Is this a new way of thinking about common prayer? If so, how would this understanding influence your participation in worship?

1 ▪ Creation and Vocation

This great God,
Like a mammy bending over her baby,
Kneeled down in the dust
Toiling over a lump of clay
Till he shaped it in his own image;
Then into it he blew the breath of life,
And man became a living soul.
Amen. Amen.

             —"The Creation" by James Weldon Johnson

Like many Americans, my family is scattered across the country. I have cousins in New Jersey, siblings in North Carolina, aunts and uncles in Georgia, and distant relatives in Virginia and Ohio. As accustomed as we have become to this distance, it was not so long ago that much of my family lived rather close to one another. My maternal and paternal families can trace their history to the Midlands and Pee Dee regions of South Carolina, to plantations where my ancestors were made into slaves by a people and a system whose vision of humanity was fractured and distorted. Like many Black families in the Deep South, my family fled from racist terror campaigns and moved to the North with the hope of economic opportunity in the middle of the twentieth century in what many historians call the "Great Migration." What carried them through the trauma of such a migration were the stories that reminded them of their identity. They were not stories of great heroism or notoriety. They were terribly uninteresting stories to those without a familial connection to them. But they were stories that continue to remind us of who we are, especially when we encounter a narrative within the larger society that speaks about the deficiency of Blackness. My great-grandparents told these stories to my grandparents, who told them to my parents, who made sure we knew them as well. If you want to know something about an individual, a community, or a people, ask them to tell you a story.

The Church, too, is a community of stories. Like my biological family, the Church is given the task of safeguarding sacred memory, of passing down the stories that matter, of regularly reminding God's people who we really are when the rest of our society attempts to communicate another story about human life and purpose: stories about competing for and acquiring material goods often at the expense of other human beings. Our liturgical life is, in some respect, stories in motion. When we listen and respond, sing and proclaim, genuflect and kneel, take and give, we are rehearsing the sacred memory of the Church over and over again. This is to say that our liturgy is itself rooted in a collection of sacred stories, what we call the Holy Bible. The collection of poems, prophecy, and prose fashioned over centuries of wandering, pilgrimage, triumph and suffering, oppression and injustice, is replete with recollections of a *shared* sacred memory. When the Church hears these sacred stories in the context of the liturgy, we are quite literally being saturated in the love of God.

To understand the Church's vocation of reconciliation, and the way the Church enacts this ministry liturgically, it is important to understand the story that grounds our existence as human beings: the Creation. The word "human" comes from a Latin word related to the word *humus,* meaning "of the earth, earthy." The first story of scripture begins with the creation of human beings from the dust of the earth, and so it is to that story we turn.

The Church exists within the longer trajectory of God's salvation plan that begins, according to the witness of Holy Scriptures, "in the beginning." As the first of the creation stories in Genesis unfolds, we witness the wonderful creation of the diverse tableau of all that is: the sun and moon, mountains and seas, plants and animals. God speaks it all into existence and calls it "good." On the sixth day, we witness the creation of humanity, who, unlike the rest of Creation, is created in God's image. Rabbi Shai Held asserts that to be created in God's image has at least two relevant implications. First, humans share in God's rule over creation (Held, *The Heart of Torah,* 1:7). This first meaning is a matter of vocation. According to Genesis 1, human beings were created to cultivate God's good creation and enable it to continue to be fruitful and productive. The second implication, connected to the vocational identity of the first, is that if humans are created to share in God's "rule" of creation, we are all equal in the eyes of God and one another. Rabbi Held suggests that this second implication "is a repudiation of the idea . . . that some people are simply meant to rule over others" (1:8).

The first creation story in Genesis 1 is often overlooked in favor of the second because the first contains words like "subdue" and "dominion." I want to retain the word "rule" and our focus on the first story because I think there is value to reclaiming it and recasting it in God's image. God is sovereign, Creation is God's dominion, and the Psalms suggest that "righteousness and justice are the foundations of God's throne." Furthermore, Rabbi Held's interpretation of Genesis 1 suggests that to "rule" in God's imagination is to enable abundance and fruitfulness through the establishment of justice and harmony. The Book of Common Prayer supports this interpretation in the catechism where it suggests that to be created in the image of God means, among other things "to live in harmony with creation" (Book of Common Prayer, 845). The prayer for the "Conservation of Natural Resources" in the prayer book also seeks to correct a gross misinterpretation of Genesis by offering the following language: "Almighty God, in giving us dominion over things on earth, you made us fellow workers in your creation: Give us wisdom and reverence so to use the resources of nature, that no one may suffer from our abuse of them, and that generations yet to come may continue to praise you for your bounty" (Book of Common Prayer, 827).

If scripture and our tradition are any indication, it would seem that the goodness of Creation was placed in the hands of God's human stewards whose vocational faithfulness would ensure its perpetual fruitfulness and abundance.

Except, that isn't what happened.

The second creation story, beginning in Genesis 2, narrates the cause of sin: humans wanted to "be like God" thus, tragically, abandoning their vocation. The loss of vocation seems to reintroduce chaos into God's ordered Creation. This unfaithfulness has natural as well as spiritual implications. First, humans are exiled from the Garden of Eden, thus representing the estrangement between human beings and God. Second, the humans are told that more effort would be required in a less productive Creation. This is not punishment in the way we often conceive of it. The first humans aren't expelled from the Garden because of some arbitrary, divine edict; rather, the first humans are expelled from the Garden because their choice to turn from God came with a consequence: God allowed them to inherit the world created by their choices. It is not the romantic definition of love we often want, but it is the definition of love that we see in God. We were created to live freely in the world God had created or we could exchange that freedom for slavery to our own ambition and live in the world we create. There is a great lesson here both in the vocational power given to humanity by God and the consequences that come along with the abuse of that power. In one choice, humanity falls from union with God to alienation, from abundance to subsistence living. This story envisions the human condition as one wherein we often live beneath our intended vocation as human beings.

The word vocation is often seen solely or primarily in either ordered ministry in the Church or in work that brings an ultimate sense of fulfillment. It is a shame that we often automatically associate the word "vocation" with "ordination" because in the human vocation, the latter understanding is truer. The human vocation is not somehow outside of human identity. It is precisely the opposite!

Our human vocation is to live into our being created in the image of the God, to share with God in the faithful rule and stewardship of Creation. We can experience this in small ways (and perhaps not-so-small ways) in our lives here and now; but, the promise is that in God's future, human beings will be fully restored to their place in Creation according to God's divine plan. When this happens, we will experience the full effects of God's reconciliation, namely the restoration of God's heaven-and-earth reality.

The word "reconcile" means "to bring back together." To "reconcile," we must first possess an image of what has been torn apart and why. Biblically and theologically, what has been torn apart is "God's heaven-and-earth reality" expressed in the harmony and abundance of the Garden of Eden. The Bible is filled with prophecies and poems, each attempting to describe with great artistic flourish God's intention for Creation. Micah tells us that in God's vision for Creation, "all shall sit under their own vines and under their own fig trees, and no one shall make them afraid" (Micah 4:4). Isaiah speaks of lions and lambs lying together, tables overflowing with food, and food for everyone who hungers (Isa. 11:6). Centuries later, John the Revelator would describe a glorious, glittering city on a bright river with fruitful trees on its banks. Humans across the centuries have yearned for a future that is abundant and fruitful. Our tradition instructs us that this yearning is rooted in a collective, albeit distant, experience of abundance connected to our human vocation as stewards of this abundance. At the heart of reconciliation then is a restoration of humanity to its full vocation—to steward, to share, and to praise.

The full expression of human nature was lost when human beings turned away from our collective vocation. As scripture imagines it, healing and reconciliation aren't simply choices. The rupture runs deeper than individual or even collective choices. The rupture has something to do with the evil powers that have been unleashed into the world as a result of human unfaithfulness. Paul describes such powers as "the rulers . . . the authorities . . . the cosmic powers of this present darkness . . . the spiritual forces of evil in the heavenly places" (Eph. 6:12). For Creation to fulfill its divine purpose, the full expression of human nature must be restored. When human beings live beneath this vocation, we see evidence of the exploitation, the abuse of one another, and the degradation of the Creation. The call for Christians is to show up for the Creation in ways that are sustainable, life-giving, nurturing, and creative.

Human Nature Restored

The Christian faith teaches us that the full expression of human nature was restored in the Messiah, Jesus Christ. The Prayer Book Collect "Of the Incarnation" says: "O God, who wonderfully created, and yet more wonderfully restored, the dignity of human nature: Grant that we may share the divine life of him who humbled himself to share our humanity, your Son Jesus Christ; who lives and reigns with you, in the unity of the Holy Spirit, one God, for ever and ever. Amen" (Book of Common Prayer, 252).

Jesus's whole ministry is one of reconciliation. He is the literal reconciliation in the flesh. Colossians tells us that "in him all the fullness of God was pleased to dwell, and through him God was pleased to reconcile to himself all things, whether on earth or in heaven, by making peace through the blood of his cross" (Col. 1:19–20). To restore human nature, God entered it, hallowed it, and demonstrated through it what the human vocation looks like. In Jesus, we are the human vocation embodied: Life is lived to its fullest, sickness and disease are healed, Creation is cared for and abundant, evil forces are banished, and even death is overthrown. We see all of this demonstrated in the healing, reconciling, feeding, and liberating work of Jesus, often called "miracles"—"signs of wonder"—that point to the presence of the kingdom of God and the incredible power of the full human vocation seen in Jesus.

These "signs of wonder" draw so much attention in the life and ministry of Jesus because they exist in a broader context where human beings are living *apart* from their full humanity. The feeding of the multitudes found in the synoptic Gospels is particularly jarring because the people are so hungry. The healing of the sick and diseased is especially startling, not only because of the illnesses themselves, but also how the broader society treats those who are ill, sick, or disabled. Even the resurrection of Jesus is made ever more remarkable because it occurs within the context of a rigorously efficient system of death that was Roman crucifixion.

To borrow from the poetic prologue of John's Gospel, the wondrous works of Jesus are light shining in the darkness, revealing just how dangerous and cruel the darkness really is. It is important to note here that "darkness" for John is not about pigmentation but

8

visibility. Harmful practices, behaviors, and systems flourish in the proverbial darkness because we cannot identify them, *we cannot see their victims*, or see the ways they are interconnected and draw their power from common sources of human shame, brokenness, and self-ishness. The light allows us to see them for what they are, to name them, and then to engage them on our way to freedom from them.

When we witness the darkness of our own time, whether that darkness is experienced personally as grief or suffering, communally as systemic oppression or exploitation, or globally as war or eco-logical disaster, we are reminded of our collective need for recon-ciliation. Though humans are certainly not to blame for earthquakes and tornadoes, the witness of our faith as demonstrated in our sacred stories is this: Our experience of Creation does not match God's dream for it. The distance between our experience of Crea-tion and God's dream for it resembles the distance between the human condition and the human vocation.

It is precisely into this space that the Gospel's call is clearest. The Gospel is not an invitation for the culturally, socially, politi-cally, and economically comfortable to amass more comfort nor it is a sacred baptism of the secular status quo. The Gospel is an invitation to die to a world that is enamored of degradation, dis-crimination, and death and rise into a world whose foundations are "eternal in the heavens" (2 Cor. 5:1). It is a call to a cross-shaped life, one which stands awkwardly and uncomfortably in the face of those who can't be bothered to see the immense pain and suf-fering in our world, and one which stands as a sign of hope, as divine solidarity with those who are the crucified in our own world.

The Gospel call is not a call to escape this world, but rather to participate in its salvation.

Reconciliation as God's Mission and the Church's Vocation

The Church is called to enter this space, to proclaim the Resurrection and its effects in Creation: namely reconciliation in the form of new Creation, and to recruit and nurture communities who commit to living the way of life that this new Creation demands, a way of life shaped by the life of Jesus. That is our work within God's mission. It is not our job to reconcile the world to God or to bring about the fullness of the kingdom of God. Pain and suffering have often resulted, particularly among the poor and marginalized, whenever powerful human beings have sought to build the kingdom of God in their image. Our work is to proclaim its reality in word and deed and then, empowered and animated by the Spirit of God, to live it because we believe it is true. This means, among other things, living a cross-shaped life where the suffering we experience due to the dissonance that exists between our experience of this world and God's dream for it serves as an entry point, where the grace of God enters our world anew and afresh.

The effects of this understanding of vocation cannot be overstated. The temptation is ever present to imagine that reconciliation is nothing more than an individual's private relationship with God alone. "Get right with God and all is good." N.T. Wright calls this kind of religion "unbiblical" and a "detached spirituality" (Wright, *The Day the Revolution Began*, 35). He claims that the Church's Gospel witness is imperiled when it makes the "three-layered mistake" of assuming that the end of the Christian story is first, the removal of faithful souls from the earth to a disembodied heaven; second, the tragic mistake of viewing the Christian life as the pursuit of moral purity rather than vocational faithfulness; and, third, developing distorted views of God and Jesus and our relationship to them (147). This kind of faith not only does damage to the Church's core theological convictions by denying the connective tissue that binds us one to another, it also does damage to those around us in repeating the words of the Gospel without the behavioral changes they call for. When the Church stands up for reconciliation in theory and yet fails to show up where human beings are in most need of it, the marginalized continue to suffer abuse—only this time, their suffering takes place under the "sacred canopy" of religion.

The Gospel call of the Church invites us to a different, radically embodied, vulnerable place because that's where reconciliation and healing occur. To step into the work that reconciliation demands, the Church must first reconcile its words and deeds. We can no longer go on with our liturgical and religious life proclaiming realities that our social, political, and economic lives continue to deny. When a religious leader comes to Jesus and asks him what he must do to inherit eternal life, Jesus has him recite the core conviction of the Jewish faith: "You shall love the Lord your God with all your heart, and with all your soul, and with all your strength, and with all your mind; and your neighbor as yourself" (Luke 10:27). Among many other things, I hear this as a call to integrity. How we think must shape how we feel, and how we feel must shape how we behave, and all of that must inspire our ethical and moral commitments to our neighbor.

I am reminded of churches who have acted upon our shared sacred memory: the Church of St. Gregory of Nyssa in San Francisco where the celebration of the Bread of Life in the Eucharist has drawn the parish to feed those who struggle with hunger and food insecurity; the Church of the Common Ground in Atlanta that offers the Word of Life and the Bread of Life to those who live on the streets; or the Common Cathedral in Boston where the celebration of the liturgy leads to ministry among the many homeless—and the countless parishes that are trying to hold open and hospitable space where connection, conversation, and even reconciliation can take place among people divided by political and ideological differences.

Reconciliation and healing are at the heart of the core identity of the Church. We are the community of people who have been reconciled and made new by our participation in the divine life of Jesus Christ. This newness summons us then to work for the renewal of the world by living the kind of life the renewed world demands. We have been healed to heal others; we have been reconciled to work for the reconciliation of the world one to another. We are those who have been given a glimpse of the destiny of humanity, a destiny that even now stirs and bubbles up among us, and must therefore work to help other people see the ramifications of this new world.

Reconciliation and healing are not only liturgical rites of the Church; they are the essence of the mission of God and the vocation of the Church. To the degree that we experience them in the liturgical life of the assembly, we are called to demonstrate them in our lives as reconciled reconcilers, those who hear and faithfully respond to our shared sacred memories, those who know, practice, and believe that the way things are need not be the way they will always be.

Reflection Questions

1. Where do you experience the abundance and beauty of Creation? Where do you experience little beauty in Creation? Where does human behavior factor into the loss of Creation's beauty or ability to flourish?

2. When you consider the "human vocation," who or what comes to mind? What about those things helps you deepen your understanding of what it means to be fully human?

3. In speaking about his own ministry, Jesus tells his disciples, "Very truly, I tell you, the one who believes in me will also do the works that I do and, in fact, will do greater works than these . . ." (John 14:12). What might this mean in terms of helping us understand the vocation of being human?

2 ▪ Baptism and the Emergence of Humanity

A crown is placed over our heads
that for the rest of our lives we are trying to grow tall enough
to wear.

—Howard Thurman

I can vividly and fondly remember the day I was baptized. It was the winter of 1995 and I was eight years old. In the language of my Baptist upbringing, I had gone forward during the altar call and accepted Jesus Christ as my Lord and Savior a few months before. Actually, to tell the story more accurately, my mother convinced me to do so. Unlike my siblings, I actually liked going to church. There was something about it that I couldn't quite find the language to describe, an inner yearning steadily drawing me to the gathered fellowship of God's people. On the actual day of the baptism itself, I remember the Church mothers huddled in the front rows of the church, dressed in all white, bedecked with glittering broaches and crowns—fanciful hats Black women traditionally wore to church that would rival the finest royal diadems of the Queen of England. I had taken the classes my church offered, though they were clearly aimed at candidates much older than I was at the time. I didn't quite understand what happened during the baptism. Even still, everything about that moment showed me that something important was going on. With all those thoughts and more swirling around my head, I took my pastor's hand and stepped into the chilly water of our baptismal pool. Before I knew it, I was taken under the water and into a life I could never have dreamed of.

To understand healing and reconciliation, we must first understand baptism. Before we proceed further, by "understand baptism," I do not mean to imply that it is in any way possible to completely excavate and exhaust the endless layers of meaning that are bound up in baptism. Baptism is the mystery from which the Church springs; it is the endless well of meaning and energy that animates the Church's work in the world. By "understand baptism," I simply mean that we must seek out what the Church is attempting to communicate in this sacramental ritual. There is a reason why the Book of Common Prayer 1979 centers holy baptism as the source of Christian faith and life. It is the thing that makes us part of the Church and the source of our authority to act in this world on God's behalf. As the apostle Paul writes, "For we do not proclaim ourselves; we proclaim Jesus Christ as Lord and ourselves as your slaves for Jesus' sake" (2 Cor. 4:5). We can proclaim Christ because in holy baptism we are made one with Christ.

Baptism is meaningful. The New Testament and several other writings from the earliest years of the Church express the many meanings of this rite of Christian initiation: the forgiveness of sins; incorporation into the one body of the Christian community; being sealed by the Spirit and marked as Christ's own; new birth;

intimate union with Christ; and participating in his death and Resurrection—to name a few. When we experience holy baptism, we experience all of this meaning and more.

Though each of these interpretations offers a helpful lens through which we can best understand baptism and what it means to be a Christian, they all have at least one thing in common: mission. We are a people called to engage in God's mission. Our sins are forgiven, thus enabling us to live reconciled to God. We are initiated into the Christian community, a people called to continue the healing work of Christ in this and every age. We are sealed as belonging to God, not as lords over each other. We are called to be servants, a way of life not taught to us by our culture. We participate in Christ's death and resurrection: that is, we are called to die to the values and practices of this age that are at odds with the Gospel of Jesus Christ, and rise into his Way of Life in the world.

And let's be realistic: the Church has often found it difficult to live into this depth of meaning. For centuries, baptism was closely linked to national or ethnic affiliation. For many today, baptism is little more than a social obligation or a talisman to ward off divine retribution. If the Church is to recover its vocation, we must recover a robust understanding of baptism along with its interlocking moral, ethical, and political claims. Among other things, baptism cannot mean national or ethnic affiliation, because, as Paul reminds us in Galatians, "all of you are one in Christ Jesus" (Gal. 3:28). Baptism brings us into the fellowship of a reconciled, transnational, transracial, transethnic community. It's not that our identities are erased. Rather, our identities are given new meaning in the light of the Resurrection. Whereas the world ascribes political and social value to our differences, in Christ we are shown a new, more equitable and compassionate way of living and moving in the world.

Baptism and God's Mission

Baptism took on new meaning and energy for me when I began to understand the mission of God and the vocation of the Church. Up to that point, I was tied to the less interesting yet somehow more frightening understanding of holy baptism as the sole way to avoid eternal punishment in hell, what some have called "celestial fire insurance." I had grown up believing one thing: that baptism was my ticket into heaven. With that understanding of baptism, I grew up thinking that my work as a follower of Jesus Christ was to do the best I could to stay out of trouble, since different kinds of trouble could imperil my fragile salvation. My other role as a baptized person was to get as many other people as I could to buy into this understanding of salvation or risk eternal damnation. One has to wonder: What image of God rests behind this fearful scenario?

This type of faith works for many people in our nation and around the globe, but it stopped working for me a long time ago. Baptism as "celestial fire insurance" stopped working for me when I began to think seriously about the implications of this understanding, particularly when I saw how this claim was used against marginalized and vulnerable people. I also found this version of the gospel would turn to ash in my mouth whenever I tried to tell others about it. Whatever life it once had was long gone in my early adulthood. I was given the sacred task of putting my faith back together again.

At some point, baptism went from fleeing divine punishment to running towards divine love. I can actually name the geographic location where this transformation occurred: the corner of Peachtree and Trinity in downtown Atlanta, Georgia. This obscure corner just down the street from the Georgia State Capitol and Atlanta City Hall is where Church of the Common Ground used to rent a storefront. The location is the geographical equivalent of the third chapter of the Gospel of Luke where the Word of God bypassed all the powerful, wealthy, and highly visible individuals and fell into the mouth of a homeless prophet named John. This grace-filled contemporary community of individuals experiencing homelessness, drug and alcohol addiction, poverty, and hunger taught me what a faithful response to divine love looked like. Each Sunday afternoon at our outdoor Eucharist, I witnessed this community of folks from whom the harshness of life and the cruelty of society had taken everything still willingly give what they had to God. They were incredibly aware of how dependent their lives were on God's grace and they weren't afraid to show it.

This community also taught me about mission. By "mission," I do not mean charity initiatives, outreach projects, or even advocacy focused on poverty and housing—though each of these is good and necessary. By "mission," I mean the work that God is doing to heal our broken world. When we would gather—whether it was for a Sunday Eucharist or a Monday afternoon foot clinic or a Wednesday morning Bible Study or a Thursday afternoon support group meeting—I saw God stitching together the fraying fabric of human relationships. It was in the tightness of this community that I glimpsed something of God's plan for Creation. It was in this space that I saw the Church really be the Church. Close. Tight. Vulnerable. Willing. Supportive. Open. Trusting. Trustworthy. Loving.

Baptism is fundamental to understanding reconciliation and healing because it is what initiates us into the reconciling and healing community of God. Baptism can mean more, but it certainly does not mean any less. When the Church has engaged baptism merely as a rite of affiliation, rather than one of initiation and transformation, we often find ourselves bearing the uncomfortable burden of the status quo. Though we might spend our entire lives struggling to grow into it, baptism is about being transformed into Christ who is the full expression of humanity. C.S. Lewis reminds us that "If we let [God]—for we can prevent Him, if we choose—he will make the feeblest and filthiest of us into a god or goddess, a dazzling, radiant, immortal creature, pulsating all through with such energy and joy and wisdom and love as we cannot now imagine, a bright stainless mirror which reflects back to God perfectly (though, of course, on a smaller scale) His own boundless power and delight and goodness" (Lewis, *Mere Christianity*, 163).

How then does baptism shine a new light on the work of healing and reconciliation? For a moment, let us think about Lewis's metaphor of humans becoming mirrors. Let us also recall the fundamental human vocation of reflecting the justice of God into Creation and reflecting Creation's praise back to God. To reconcile and heal is to restore our ability to reflect God's glory and Creation's praise. Wherever human action or inaction prevents God's justice from being experienced, wherever sickness or disease prevent us from experiencing a fulsome life and thus prevent us from adequately reflecting the Creation's praise to God, wherever human relationships prevent the love of God from being made manifest in our world, that is precisely where healing and reconciliation are needed. Rowan Williams reminds us that baptism places us squarely in the neighborhood of Jesus, "but Jesus is found in the neighborhood of human confusion and suffering, defenselessly alongside those in need. If being baptized is being led to where Jesus is, then being baptized is being led towards the chaos and the neediness of humanity that has forgotten its own destiny" (Williams, *Being Christian*, 5).

Baptized into God's Mission

These issues are not merely a matter of theory. Our world is in desperate need of healing. As I write these words, the United States of America is at yet another moment of reckoning with its past and present practice of White Supremacy. While millions stood up to protest the killing of George Floyd in Minneapolis, Minnesota, the hard work of reconciliation still lies ahead of us. Add to this the ongoing political climate where the widening ideological gap between Democrats and Republicans results in attempted dismantling of democracy and leaves our body susceptible to political exploitation, corruption, and abuse. Add to this the global health crisis known as COVID-19. Each of these alone would be more than enough to signal a need for healing. Add them all together and we can sense an urgent, divine, prophetic call to be about the work God has called us to.

I never saw the video of George Floyd's murder. I have seen enough Black people killed on tape to last me several lifetimes. I could not bring myself to watch one more. Even still, the feelings all came rushing back from six summers ago, when Michael Brown was shot in Ferguson, Missouri. All at once I felt afraid, anxious, hopeless, sad, and angry. But this time, a new feeling sat alongside the rest: resolve. In the years since Michael Brown was killed, I have been able to clarify my sense of call as a Christian and as a priest, and I have been able to contribute to the world of racial reconciliation and healing. I've taught courses, given lectures, organized marches, written books and blogs, and led workshops. I've also sat across the table from people who told me that "Black Lives Matter" is akin to a terrorist group or have flat-out denied the existence of structural racism in a society where the phrase "all men are created equal" only applied to white, landowning men when it was first penned in 1776. Each workshop, each cup of coffee, each blog post, and each hard conversation has helped to heal the world in some small way. Whenever despair crept in, I would remind myself of the oft-quoted statement from the Jewish Mishna: "You are not obligated to complete the work, but neither are you free to desist from it."

One such conversation happened a few weeks after George Floyd was killed. I was invited by the local police chief to facilitate a conversation between the chief and a group of local activists. What prompted the invitation was a volatile encounter at a local gas station: a white woman was accused of attempting to run over a group of Black Lives Matter protesters after the protesters surrounded her car. Local law enforcement intervened and permitted the woman to go home. The event went viral, with protesters suggesting that they would not be treated the same if the situation were reversed. In the weeks between the initial incident and the conversation, both groups had been on the receiving end of less than charitable depictions by the other in local print and social media. As we often do in our society, we assume the negative intent of the other even before we actually meet them, thus dooming our attempts at reconciliation before they even begin. This conversation was laden with anxiety before it got off the ground.

As the conversation unfolded, however, I could see a greater sense of understanding coming from those in the room. Each person listened intently to the other and reflected on what was being shared. Both parties shared their experiences and owned up to their unfair characterizations of the other. The conversation was supposed to last 60 minutes, but after 90 minutes, the police chief had his assistant cancel his next few meetings. His reasoning? "This is too important." During one of the more fascinating parts of the conversation, participants talked about how easily it is for symbols to be misused and misinterpreted. "What we need," said one of the activists, "is clarity rooted in relationship."

As the conversation found its natural conclusion almost ninety minutes after it was originally scheduled to end, I shared that it had been an honor to be in the room, but that my presence was not needed for future gatherings. Both parties found ways of communicating honestly and respectfully across an ever-widening chasm of difference. I also shared that there was much work left to be done, but that much had been accomplished in that one meeting. We left the local police department and went our separate ways with the nation still reeling from George Floyd's horrifying death, but this community just a little closer.

I realize that it was my status as an ordained person that gave me access to that room. That said, I didn't accept it because of the hands that were placed on my head. I accepted the invitation because of the Spirit that had taken up residence in my heart. In the weeks leading up to that moment, I had begun praying the "Prayer Attributed to Saint Francis" each day:

> Lord, make us instruments of your peace. Where there is hatred, let us sow love; where there is injury, pardon; where there is discord, union; where there is doubt, faith; where there is despair, hope; where there is darkness, light; where there is sadness, joy. Grant that we may not so much seek to be consoled as to console; to be understood as to understand; to be loved as to love. For it is in giving that we receive; it is in pardoning that we are pardoned; and it is in dying that we are born to eternal life. Amen.
>
> —Book of Common Prayer, 833

Being a part of that difficult conversation was one way I thought I could be an instrument of God's peace. I wasn't there to get anyone to understand my experience or perspective; rather, I wanted to be open to hear the experiences of others: local youths who felt targeted by the police department and police officers who felt victimized by unfair generalizations. It is easy to slip into an unhelpful "both sides" argument, and many do. I do know that the call to reconcile is a call to stand between two opposing realities and bring them together by helping them imagine and create a new world together, one where mercy and truth meet together.

In the months since that conversation, I have reflected on what kept me in that room. Lesslie Newbigin writes that "the deepest motive for mission is simply the desire to be with Jesus where he is, on the frontier between the reign of God and the usurped dominion of the devil." What kept me in that room is what ought to keep each of us in that hard place of faith when the stakes are high and where the instinct to surrender is strong: a desire to be with Jesus. Baptism fills us with a waterborne desire to build bridges across the chasms of human pain. The closer we come to Jesus Christ, the more we want to do what he does and live the kind of life he lives, one where we enter the rooms of our supposed enemies to disrupt the whole enemy enterprise altogether.

Reflection Questions

1. If you, the reader, have been baptized, what do you remember about your baptism? What has been told to you about your baptism? What impact has being baptized had in your life?

2. The Five Baptismal Promises all flow from our faith expressed in the words of the Apostles' Creed. In the context of our reflection on reconciliation and healing, where do you see these themes present in the Baptismal Covenant? What aspects of reconciliation and healing are *not* reflected in the Covenant?

3. Rowan Williams suggests that baptism brings us into close proximity to Jesus who is to be found where humanity is most in need. What people come to mind when you hear this? What practices or behaviors reveal this to you?

3 ▪ The Reconciliation of a Penitent

Once a man is united to God, how could he not live forever?
Once a man is separated from God, what can he do but wither
and die?

—C.S. Lewis

One of the fundamental theological convictions at the heart of the Christian faith is the deep and abiding sense that Creation simply does not work the way the Creator designed it to work and that this "malfunction" has some impact on the human condition. Throughout the course of Jewish and Christian history, this observation has been described in different ways, perhaps most famously by Augustine of Hippo in the fourth century as "original sin." The recognition of a "malfunction" in Creation is not intended to deny its fundamental goodness. Augustine affirms it multiple times in his *Confessions*. Recognizing the problem is an attempt to plot a new course forward. Consider the Hebrew prophet, Ezekiel, who diagnosed the problem as residing in the human heart. God gives Ezekiel the following word, "A new heart I will give you, and a new spirit I will put within you; and I will remove from your body the heart of stone and give you a heart of flesh" (Ezek. 36:26).

Part of the wisdom held in the Jewish scriptures is the desire of God to be with the people of God held alongside the heartbreaking reality that the behavior of the people of God continued to make that difficult if not impossible at times. According to Genesis, God created by ordering and structuring the chaotic darkness. The problem seems to arise when humans pushed against the divine order and reintroduced chaos. The book of Leviticus, oft maligned and misunderstood in Christian contexts, is not merely a list of arcane rules and ritual practices. It is a book in which we see God's people working out what it means to be with God, specifically what conditions would make that reunion possible. At the heart of the book is the creation of space—the tabernacle—where the order of God is legislated and enforced such that God's holy and life-giving presence is able to abide there in the midst of God's people. God says as much in Exodus when he instructs Moses to ask the people to contribute to the construction of the tabernacle, "so that I may dwell among them" (Exod. 25:8). God's presence is a presence marked by order rather than destabilizing chaos.

As humans, we experience the resurgence of chaos in various ways. We experience it globally in wars that devastate and displace generations of people as well as in ecological disasters that disrupt the inherent beauty infused into God's Creation. Closer to home, we experience the resurgence of chaos in our own nation in the hyperpolarization that makes governing impossible, in the ongoing struggle against White Supremacy and for racial healing and justice, in the prevalence of poverty that robs human beings of dignity and life that is the birthright of every one of us. We also experience this resurgence of chaos personally, in the experience and pain of aging and diminishing bodies, in struggles with mental illness, in the interpersonal conflicts and tragedies that have the capacity to slowly drain our lives of joy and fullness. However we experience the chaos, we can each attest to its reality and our struggle to break free from it.

Christianity responds to the existential question presented to us by the resurgence of chaos in God's ordered and therefore "very good" creation—reconciliation. Baptism is the moment where we are given the heart of God. Although it is easy to make baptism all about becoming the member of a particular church, baptism is not about church membership. Baptism is about incorporation into the body, the life, the death, and the heart of Christ. When we are baptized, we respond to God's "yes" with a yes of our own, choosing to give our lives away to God who then makes us new over the course of our lives such that we reflect more of God's presence in the world, thus participating in God's mission. This is because the saving work of Jesus Christ is at the heart of baptism. In Jesus Christ, what was distorted and disrupted in Creation is recast anew. The long exile of humanity, demonstrated in miniature by the exile of the Jewish people from the Promised Land, has been reversed by God's decisive and divine action. It is true that the full effects of this reconciliation have yet to be felt across the full Creation. This is the essence of the Christian hope: that one day, the reconciliation we experience in small, yet real ways, will be experienced fully in the great and final day.

In the meantime, the work of Christian people is to partner with God in the divine ordering of chaos. As we explored in the previous chapter, the Christian vocation takes us precisely where chaos is most acute in order that we might proclaim and practice the reconciling, ordering, and life-giving Gospel of Jesus Christ. It is important to remember that the Christian rites and rituals we experience personally must also participate in what God has done and is doing globally and cosmically. Liturgy is mission and mission is liturgy.

This interplay between the personal and the cosmic is helpful in our exploration of the rite for the "Reconciliation of a Penitent," or what is traditionally and culturally known as the rite of "confession." From the onset, the title is important here. When we refer to the rite as "confession," we place the emphasis in the wrong place: with the act of confession. The emphasis of the rite ought to be with God's divine action: the reconciliation of the penitent. This might seem like an insignificant matter of semantics, but it really has a lot to do with what we understand to be happening ritually and whether we can grasp the broader implications of the rite itself. Like many of the sacraments of the Church, it is easy to make them so much about us that it impoverishes our experience of them beyond us. It is not simply that we confess and God forgives. It is that, much like the Father in the Parable of the Prodigal, God's forgiveness beats us to the punch and if God can be so prodigal with forgiveness and reconciliation, perhaps we are called to do the same for others.

The prayer book catechism tells us that "reconciliation of a penitent" is among five "sacramental rites" developed by the Church under the guidance of the Holy Spirit. The term "sacramental rites" is attempt to draw a distinction between the two major sacraments of holy baptism and holy Eucharist, which developed in the first generation of the Church, and the other five sacramental rites, which were developed by the Church through history. Lee Mitchell and Ruth Meyers remind us that the ministry of reconciliation, while spoken of later as a "sacrament," "has its roots in the gospel and in the reconciling ministry of Jesus Christ" (Mitchell and Meyers, *Praying Shapes Believing*, 235). Not only has the Church always seen reconciliation as core to its vocation, it has always made space for repentance and reconciliation in the lives of the faithful. The catechism further reminds us that it is the work of all baptized people to continue "Christ's work of reconciliation in the world" (Book of Common Prayer, 855). The reconciling life begins when we are reconciled to God by first sharing in the saving work of Jesus Christ by way of baptism and is strengthened through our continued participation in that work through ongoing engagement with the local eucharistic fellowship—the Church.

Although Mitchell and Meyers helpfully remind us that "living the baptismal and eucharistic life is itself a ministry of reconciliation," the Prayer Book rites for reconciliation provide an opportunity for personal confession and forgiveness (Mitchell and Meyers, 236). There are simply times in each of our lives when our experience of estrangement and distance from God and one another is such that we must avail ourselves of the opportunity to participate more intentionally in the Church's practice of reconciliation.

Sin and Reconciliation

It is worth pausing here and noting how the prayer book talks about sin. It is a shame that we so often experience sin stretched out of shape. Many experience the word "sin" as an endless list of moral taboos, like gambling, gossiping, or drunkenness. As a gay person who grew up in the church, I experienced the word "sin" as a cudgel wielded against my sense of self-worth. These and other experiences of the word are unfortunate and often result in us turning away from God's grace in the moment we need it most. One of the most important tasks of the Church in this moment of transformation and renewal is to clarify what we mean when we use certain words. For example, our doctrine of sin is not about sin itself; rather, we talk about sin to enable us to return to God and inherit the kind of world God desires for us to inherit. Sin isn't the point: reconciliation is.

The catechism tells us that "sin is the seeking of our own will instead of the will of God, thus distorting our relationship with God, with other people, and with all creation" (Book of Common Prayer, 848). When seen this way, the unhelpful conceptions of sin as either a list of moral taboos or as a weapon melt away and are instead replaced by a definition that attempts to diagnose the problem at the core of the human condition. Mitchell and Meyers help us to see that sin is a "disease of the will" (Mitchell and Meyers, 240). Augustine of Hippo called sin a disordering or misuse of the gift of love (Augustine, *City of God*, XV.22). As Paul confessed, "For I do not do the good I want, but the evil I do not want is what I do" (Rom. 7:19). The wisdom inherited from our

32

Jewish siblings and accumulated through the Christian tradition suggest that the divine gift of freewill has been corrupted by sin, thus making it more difficult to make the choices we know are right for ourselves and for others.

The rite of confession provides us with an opportunity to carry those vulnerable parts of ourselves and lay them before the searching and saving gaze of our gracious God. The drama of this moment should not be overlooked. Julia Gatta and Martin Smith remind us that "saying our sins out loud makes them real to us and deepens our penitence. At the same time, it helps us unburden ourselves and hand these sins over to the mercy of God. Pent up, anguishing memories are released as we communicate them to another and let them go" (Gatta and Smith, *Go in Peace*, 30). A piece of wisdom embedded in liturgical action is the effect of embodying the action itself. Whatever else might be said about the ritual, naming the most vulnerable parts of ourselves, hearing God's forgiveness laser-focused on our deepest guilt and shame, and consenting to the forgiving touch of the Church dramatizes and therefore deepens our understanding and experience of God's grace. Liturgy is parable in motion.

Part of what we are is dramatized in the rite for reconciliation is what it means to return to God. When we are baptized, we promise to "persevere in resisting evil and, whenever you fall into sin, repent and return to the Lord" (Book of Common Prayer, 304). It is worth noting here that the question is not if you fall into sin, but when. Built into our tradition is the reality that the ongoing Christian life is one where we continue to struggle against the prevalence of evil. As previously mentioned, the full effects of the reconciliation wrought by the death and resurrection of Jesus Christ have not been implemented across the entire Creation. Instead, those of us who have been renewed in baptism are called to struggle against evil in the light of the future that we have experienced and that we know is yet to come. In the words of N.T. Wright, "the followers of Jesus . . . must get used to living with a form of theological jetlag" (Wright, *Paul*, 222). This is because through Christ, although we live in a world that seems stuck in patterns of abuse, estrangement, violence, and harm, we have a glimpse into God's new, reconciled Creation. The rite of reconciliation presupposes a healed and reconciled world. Without this blessed hope, the rite is meaningless.

Reconciliation of a penitent is the path offered by the Church to ritualize and dramatize the return of sinners to right relationship with God, with each person serving as a representative of the larger return of Creation to right relationship with its Creator. In the prayer book, both rites place the agency of forgiveness and reconciliation with God. As Mitchell and Meyers remind us that "from beginning to end, reconciliation is the action of God whose call to repentance we respond." The divine call to repentance, to *metanoia* or a "changed mind," can be found throughout the scriptures. Repentance is not merely the act of feeling sorrow for wrongs committed or hurt caused. To repent is to endeavor to change course, to chart a new path forward. When we consider repentance against the backdrop of what we have discussed, it is possible to see that repentance allows us to see our lives for what they really are, particularly the parts of our lives where our lack of discipline or disordered love has reintroduced chaos into our lives and the lives of others around us. Reconciliation helps us to *see it* so that we can reclaim our true nature in Christ.

The Wisdom of Reconciliation

Perhaps we can now see how the wisdom of the Christian rite of reconciliation sheds light on some of the struggles we face as humans on this planet and as citizens of the United States. Our struggle against the evils of racism and White Supremacy for example call for repentance. Too many have loved power and wealth more than those also created in God's image. As a country, we must not only express sorrow and remorse for the path we have walked thus far, but we must also endeavor to chart a new path forward, one that heals and repairs the damage of past generations and sets future generations on a pathway towards peace. Clearly, this is not a simple path. Neither is it a path that can be walked absentmindedly. Rather, the path toward reconciliation present in the Christian tradition requires bravery in admitting where we have gone astray, vulnerability in admitting our fear of the road ahead, generosity in repairing the damage, and vigilance to stay the course when the road becomes tiresome and inconvenient. From a Christian standpoint, the Holy Spirit empowers us to stay the course, knowing that we are already forgiven and reconciled. The work we do is simply to bring into fruition what has already been proclaimed and prepared by Christ.

The same is true when we consider personal or private reconciliation. When we come before a priest to receive the rite of reconciliation, we come before one who stands in the stead of the entire Church. In this moment, we must demonstrate bravery in confessing the parts of our lives that demonstrate the seeking of our own will rather than that of God, which also calls to mind the damage that this causes: broken relationships, addictions, and a sense of alienation from God's grace. We must also endeavor to do what we can to repair the damage we have caused. This is not a "punishment," as is often the perception of penance. Rather, we seek to repair the damage because, as agents of God's reconciling Gospel, such actions are our charge. To be faithful witnesses of Christ whose death and resurrection reconciled us to God, we must also be reconcilers. Finally, we must rely on the power of the Holy Spirit to help us "amend" our lives and to "hereafter live a godly, righteous, and sober life" (Book of Common Prayer, 42).

Being reconciled to God invites us to respond to God's persistent call to repent by reclaiming the new life of Christ in which we were clothed in baptism, but squandered as a result of our all-too-human struggle against sin. Here again we find that reconciliation finds roots and meaning in baptism. Just like baptism, the rite of reconciliation liturgically enacts our dying and rising again with Christ. As in baptism, we are brought into the intimate embrace of the Church. "Experiencing a renewal of baptismal grace through the rite of reconciliation reinforces the truth that we sin and are forgiven as members of the community of Christ. Sin can make us excruciating lonely: public sins can estrange neighbors from us, while hidden sins can estrange us from them. In reconciliation we reach out to the church through the person of a priest, and our isolation is overcome" (Gatta and Smith, 32). Reconciliation brings us back to the God who has never abandoned us by bringing us back into the community of the faithful through whom we experience and discern the presence of God.

What we experience in the rite of reconciliation is what the entirety of the Christian faith anticipates: greater union with God. Admittedly, we still behold and experience the union with God "in a mirror, dimly" but we still hold on to the hope that we will see it "face to face" (1 Cor. 13:12). This brief moment of divine mercy captures our imaginations and then sends us back into the world set on fire with this "foretaste of glory divine." Consider for a moment the implication of a world filled with people whose human imaginations have become fixated on the reconciling presence of God. Imagine how that kind of energy would enable us to engage the chaos around us. Whether we experience reconciliation individually or corporately, if we pay attention, we have glimpsed something of our destiny. It is up to us to share that glimpse with others and to walk in the world as if what God has promised to us is already true for everyone else as well.

Reflection Questions

1. The rite of "confession" is a popular trope in movies and television shows. When have you seen the rite portrayed on screen? How does the depiction you watched compare to what has been discussed already?

2. The Anglican maxim, "all may, some should, none must," is often applied to the sacramental rite of reconciliation. What does this mean to you? Being that the Episcopal Church does not require personal and private reconciliation as a precondition for eucharistic participation, what might this demonstrate about the nature of the grace of this sacrament?

3. Have you participated in this rite? Without diverging sensitive details, can you talk about how it felt for you? If you have not participated in this rite, what has kept you away from it?

4 ▪ Ministration to the Sick

I think it is healing behavior,
to look at something so broken and see the possibility and
wholeness in it.

—Adrienne Maree Brown

I was drawn to the miracles of Jesus as a child. Jesus seemed to function like a superhero, and among his many superpowers was the ability to walk on water, multiply food, and heal the sick. I also grew up in a tradition that placed a lot of emphasis on the charismatic ministry of Jesus. Jesus was a miracle worker and true believers were those who could work miracles. Try as I might, I never really mastered the art of walking on water, although I did learn how to stretch a meal or two from my grandmother.

It wasn't until much later that my maturing understanding of the healing, reconciling, feeding, and liberating work of Jesus helped me grasp the nature of healing. When it comes to Jesus, the kingdom of God is the point, not the charismatic ministry itself. The charismatic ministry serves to point to the reality of the closeness of the kingdom. If the kingdom of God were the sun, the ministry of Jesus is the life-giving light and heat that radiate from it. To be a follower of Jesus then is not to be someone who embodies a Jesus-like charismatic ministry, but rather someone who can bear witness to the kingdom of God as Jesus did. While

I don't deny the reality of charismatic gifts like healing, I know that they only serve to remind the world that there is another world, over, under, and throughout the one we experience, a world of human potential and God's dreams. In that way, it is possible to see wholeness even in the most broken, the most damaged, the most chaotic, and the most painful places in us and in the world.

The sacramental rituals of the prayer book "work" because, among other things, they give us a glimpse into the promise of God's future. I continue the metaphor: They point to the presence of the sun even on a cloudy day. Such a vision, such an experience, propels us back into the ordinary human life with a fresh vision for what is possible. From a Christian standpoint, we see and experience God's future through the life, self-giving death, and risen life of Jesus Christ. As such, each of the sacramental rites of the church find their theological grounding in the saving work of Jesus Christ. By them and through them we participate in the life of the wounded and risen Christ. Because of them, the kingdom of God breaks into our everyday lives, consecrating the ordinary with the blessed touch of God's Holy Spirit.

It is important to note and emphasize here that God's promised future is not somehow removed from the physical reality of the world. It is precisely within the physical reality of this world that God's future finds its most compelling context. When the Son of God became human, his incarnation "restored the dignity of human nature" (Book of Common Prayer, 214). Moreover, the death and resurrection of Jesus Christ are bodily experiences. The physical world, distorted by sin, has now been restored in the risen body of Jesus Christ. It is a shame that so much of Christian tradition has displayed an ambivalence or open hostility to the human body. The incarnation demonstrates God's commitment to the wellbeing of the physical world and the human body.

What the prayer book calls "Ministration to the Sick" is one of the sacramental rites of the Church that bring God's commitment to the wellbeing of the body into fuller picture. "Holy Scripture teaches us that Jesus healed many who were sick as a sign of the reign of God come near, and sent the disciples to continue this work of healing through prayer in his name" (*Enriching our Worship 2*, 38). As with the rite for the "Reconciliation of a Penitent," the rite for "Ministration to the Sick," has roots in the Gospels. When we follow the story of Jesus, we see him as one whose very presence brought healing to those who experienced illness or suffering. The point of the healing was to serve as a sign of the nearness of the kingdom of God. Once again, we are reminded that sacraments give a glimpse into God's promised future.

What We Mean When We Say "Healing"

The prayer book presents us with a theological challenge on two fronts. First, we are challenged to develop a more holistic understanding of healing in the context of the advances and ongoing limitations of medical science. Second, whereas much of human history sees a connection between illness and divine retribution for wrongdoing, our liturgical language and action must continue to disassociate sickness from sin. John Macquarrie notes that "sin may be the cause of suffering, either in the perpetrator . . . or in

[the] victims. People who are gluttonous or bibulous or sexually promiscuous are likely to cause damage to their own health and may cause even more suffering to others than to themselves, but that cannot be made into a general rule that sin is the cause of sickness" (*A Guide to the Sacraments*, 159–160). Some sickness is, in fact, a result of the conscious choices we make that knowingly or unknowingly bring harm to others and to us. Other times, sickness is the result of our biology or our environment over which we have little or no control. In short, healing is complicated and how we talk about should be carefully nuanced.

Mitchell and Meyers remind us that the 1928 Book of Common Prayer represented a dramatic shift from previous books in the Church's understanding of its healing ministry. Prior to the 1928 Book of Common Prayer, Anglican rites for Ministration to the Sick, and even antecedent rites, reflected the medical science of antiquity or the Middle Ages, which assumed that the sick person would likely not recover. As a result, the prayers were "for grace to accept sickness patiently and die well" (Mitchell and Meyers, 246). With the focus on death and dying, this sacramental rite was commonly referred to as the "Last Rites." The 1928 and 1979 prayer books emphasize healing much more than previous prayer books, a move that reflects the optimism born of great advances in medical science in the twentieth century.

The question about the nature of healing remains, particularly because "bodily healing . . . is notoriously undependable" (Mitchell and Meyers, 251). If the focus of the sacrament is only bodily healing, then what is the purpose of a sacrament that doesn't seem to "work" reliably? To understand the meaning of healing, we must focus our attention on the saving work of Jesus Christ, particularly as we experience and participate in holy baptism. The rite of healing unites us to the suffering, wounded, and risen of Christ through whom we come to experience Christian life. In this rite we are brought before the cross—the bodily suffering of Christ—and his risen life: that which follows death. Thus, "union with Christ in his victory over death is . . . a primary purpose of the healing ministry" of the church (Mitchell and Meyers, 253). Remember: Sacraments give us a glimpse into God's future and through faith we know that this future is open to us through the life, passion, death, and resurrection of Christ.

One of the most difficult and transforming years of my life was the year I spent as a Pastoral Resident at Emory University Hospital Midtown in Atlanta, Georgia. During that year I was dealing with immense personal struggles, attempting to navigate the vocational discernment process in the Diocese of Atlanta, and participating in a rigorous program of pastoral formation. Perhaps it was the confluence of each of these challenging streams that made this year particularly fruitful. I was assigned the seventh floor of the hospital where one would find the hospice unit, oncology unit, and intensive care unit where the most critically ill patients in the hospital received care. Rarely did patients leave the seventh floor alive.

During one of the rounds. I met a young woman who had recently been diagnosed with an aggressive form of breast cancer. Her experience changed how I thought of individuals with a cancer diagnosis. One typical image of someone struggling with the disease is physical frailty, but she seemed perfectly healthy to me. The only visible thing that gave away her illness was her presence in the hospital. She and I struck up a wonderful pastoral relationship. During her several weeks stay in the hospital, I would visit her each day. Early in her stay we would talk for hours, do puzzles, and watch daytime television.

But, then, after a few weeks I began to notice her illness. She began to sleep for longer periods and she moved slowly. Our visits, once filled with laughter and jokes, took a more somber tone. She knew from the time she was brought into the hospital that she was going to die. After a few weeks it became painfully, excruciatingly evident. During one of our last conversations, she told me tearfully that she had prayed for God to heal her but that she didn't feel like God was listening to her. In that moment I thought about how terrible that must feel, to have dedicated your life to a particular belief system only to find it unsupportive in the moment you need it most. I nodded, unsure of what to say or how to hold that space.

After a while, I opened my prayer book to Psalm 22 and began to read: "My God, my God, why have you forsaken me and are so far from my cry and from the words of my distress?" (Book of Common Prayer, 610). After reading a few more verses, she stopped me and asked me where I found this poem. I told her it was a psalm, the one Jesus prayed in the hour of his own death. I don't remember the finer details of many pastoral encounters, but I remember this one. She asked if I would pray for her and I did.

44

We grabbed each other's hands and prayed the words of a hymn she and I both knew:

> Jesus knows all about our struggles, and he will guide till the day is done. There's not a friend like the lowly Jesus.
>   No not one. No not one.

Admittedly, up to that moment, I had associated that hymn with my own personal struggles with shame, grief, or pain. During this particular conversation, I was reminded that death is also a struggle Jesus knew and knows intimately. Thomas Talley reminds us that when we recognize God's solidarity with us in our struggle with illness and death, "the passage of Christ through death to life" becomes our own (Talley, *Worship*, 55). To be healed is to be made aware of God's solidarity with suffering and death and to thus be gathered up by that spiritual energy into the life of Christ, buoyed by the knowledge that no matter what we encounter, God's promise of wholeness is with us.

From a pastoral position, the Church's work as a healing presence is keenly important. Our baptismal union with Christ does not remove us from the world of pain and sorrow. If anything, this union only highlights our experience of such. Rowan Williams reminds us that baptism draws us to those places where human pain and suffering are most acute. The ritual practice of Ministration to the Sick is utterly honest in that it honors sickness, dying, and death for what they are—real human experiences—but human experiences cast in the light of Christ's presence with us. Each person living will one day have to experience death. Ministration to the Sick is not a magic wand or shield to be wielded against death; rather, it offers us the assurance that we are not alone but rather drawn into the life of the One who will not let go of us, in life, ill health, and death.

Healing and the Mission of God

This then leads us to the missional question: How does the Church's understanding of healing and the sacramental rite of Ministration to the Sick enable the community of faith to participate in God's mission in the wider world? Let us recall a few important details. First, we take as a given that God is relentlessly pursuing the reconciliation and healing of the world. Second, the agent of a sacrament is Christ and in each sacrament we see a particular aspect of the ministry of Christ. Third, all sacraments tend toward the fullness of the kingdom of God. With each of these assumptions in mind, there are at least two ways that the sacramental rite of Ministration to the Sick enables us to participate in the mission of God. First of all, what we experience personally is in fact a foretaste of the kingdom of God. Second, the divine solidarity that we experience in Ministration to the Sick can guide the Church in its work to be a healing presence in the world. It is this second point that I'd like to explore more deeply.

As I write these pages, the world is experiencing the COVID-19 pandemic, the worst global health crisis in over a century. To date, millions have perished throughout the world with exponentially more cases of infection reported. Interestingly, the hardest hit countries are those who seemed to be the best prepared to deal with a pandemic: the industrialized, and wealthy nations of the West. In the United States alone, hundreds of thousands of people have died. The amount of suffering this pandemic has caused is difficult to overstate.

Among the various theological questions raised by the pandemic, healing is one of them. What are we to do with the immense amount of suffering being experienced by our communities? One thing that has become painfully clear is that the ongoing pandemic is highlighting the fissures that currently exist in our body politic, exacerbating existing sources of anxiety and fear. Henri Nouwen wisely wrote, "Like the Semitic nomads, we live in a desert with lonely travelers who are looking for a moment of peace, for a fresh drink, and for a sign of encouragement so that they can continue their mysterious search for freedom" (*Wounded Healer*, 95). The pandemic has greatly magnified our sense of loneliness and isolation. It is to this experience that the rite for Ministration to the Sick provides wisdom.

Let us keep in mind that Ministration to the Sick is a liturgical act. Mitchell and Meyers remind us that the service begins with these words: "Peace be to this house and all who dwell in it." This greeting makes clear that the Church's role in this ministry is beyond that of a pastoral visit (Mitchell and Meyers, 248). The primary actor in any liturgy is God who invites and initiates and we, in turn, respond to God's grace. This suggests two things. First, that our desire for healing and wholeness in ourselves and in the world is *preceded* by God's. This desire for healing and wholeness is at the heart of God's mission. When we experience situations where we desire healing, it is helpful to know that God is present in the desire itself. This again highlights God's solidarity with us in our sickness and suffering. Second, Ministration to the Sick as a ritual suggests that we are engaged in worship, in an intentional encounter with the triune God. Healing therefore happens within the context of human beings living into part of our vocation, namely to offer praise and worship to our Creator. There is an implicit connection between the source of healing and human vocation.

Another piece of wisdom contained in our liturgical rite for the Ministration to the Sick is found in the inclusion of the confession of sin. Without careful reflection, it is easy to slip into a problematic theological position that automatically places the blame of illness on the sick person. We must remember that the causes of illness are myriad. There are situations where illness is the direct result of personal choices. There are also situations where illness is the result of biological or environmental factors beyond our own control. And there are situations in which illness is caused by others who have little regard for human wellbeing. The varied nature of sickness requires a nuanced understanding of sin and reconciliation. In some instances, it might be worth pausing to ask: For what might the ill person need forgiveness? If the illness is the result of personal choices, then it would be appropriate to offer one's confession and receive God's grace and forgiveness as one navigates the ongoing complexities of illness. If, on the other hand, the illness is the result of factors beyond our control, such as biology or environment, then it might be worth asking other questions that arise around the illness. Does the often-intensified need for care during illness potentially highlight our inattentiveness to prayer and the spiritual life prior to our diagnosis? Does our illness draw attention to unjust systems of environmental exploitation that cause physical harm to others? The inclusion of the confession of sin highlights the reality that sickness often stirs up a plethora of spiritual questions and needs. When we apply this wisdom more broadly, our experience of healing as God's people within God's Creation will undoubtedly stir up deep and uncomfortable questions that will need to be confronted and held within God's grace. As Mitchell and Meyers wisely point out "forgiveness is an integral part of the healing process" (250).

The final observation I would like to make concerns the inclusion of the "church's principal healing ministries: the laying on of hands and anointing of the sick" (Mitchell and Meyers, 250). The presence of a healing, physical touch is a revolutionary act in normal times, but particularly in a time when such proximity is considered dangerous. In a time when a global pandemic is asking us to remain physically distanced from one another and when our body politic is suffering from widening ideological gaps preventing us from living peaceably with one another, perhaps the wisdom held in this part of the rite suggests something about leaning in close to one another and endeavoring to build closer, more intimate relationships with one another. To be a follower of Jesus in the midst of a fractured body politic and a global health crisis requires a commitment to live as a healing presence, to live as a person whose daily life affirms the healing presence of God in the world, the vibrant life of God that is pulsating throughout the world just below the surface.

Again, we return to the subject of baptism and what God is doing with us in that moment. When we respond to God's "yes" to us with a "yes" of our own, God heals us, not by taking us out of the messiness of human life, but by taking us through it and providing a greater context of meaning. With Christ, we are taken into obscure catacombs of the human condition only to find life in the place where we least expected to find it. Whether it is experienced in the sacramental rite for Ministration to the Sick or through an unexpected encounter with the presence of the living God, the experience of healing can become the process in which the promises of God become real to us. We discover when we are at our lowest, most hopeless moments, that the promise of God is true. When Jesus says, "I am with you, even to the end of the age," he means it. We are healed because in pain, anxiety, and suffering we discover just how close we are to Christ who bears our burdens and forgives all our sins.

Reflection Questions

1. Compare the titles "Last Rites" and "Ministration to the Sick." How do these strike you as different?

2. Consider the inclusion of the "Confession of Sin" in the rite for the "Ministration to the Sick." How is this inclusion helpful? How might it not be helpful?

3. Have you yourself or do you know someone who had a profound experience of God during an illness? What happened? What do you make of this story?

5 ■ A World Healed and Reconciled

Oh freedom!
Oh freedom!
Oh freedom over me!
And before I'd be a slave
I'll be buried in my grave
And go home to my Lord and be free.

—Negro Spiritual

On April 3, 1968, Dr. Martin Luther King Jr. took the pulpit at the historic Mason Temple Church of God in Christ in Memphis, Tennessee, to deliver what would become his last speech. He was in Memphis to support striking sanitation workers, having pivoted his work within the Civil Rights Movement to support individuals and communities struggling with poverty in what he called "The Poor People's Campaign." Throughout his life, Dr. King dedicated his energy to a vision of human relationships that were based on compassion, justice, and wellbeing.

Toward the end of this speech, Dr. King stepped completely into the prophetic tradition that served as the theological foundation of his life's work. "I've been to the mountaintop," he said. "Like anybody, I would like to live a long life. Longevity has its place. But I'm not concerned about that now. I just want to do God's will. And He's allowed me to go up to the mountain. And

I've looked over. And I've seen the Promised Land. I may not get there with you. But I want you to know tonight, that we, as a people, will get to the Promised Land. And I'm happy tonight. I'm not worried about anything. I'm not fearing any man. Mine eyes have seen the glory of the coming of the Lord" (King Jr., "I've Seen the Promised Land"). The next morning, shortly after 6:00 p.m., Dr. King was shot on the balcony of the Lorraine Motel in Memphis, Tennessee. He left behind a vision of the "Promised Land" that speaks to a world that is healed and reconciled, one I believe the Church anticipates by our ritual acts of healing and reconciliation.

A world healed and reconciled is the hope that buoys the sacred scriptures of Judaism and Christianity. This hope surely arose when the first humans experienced alienation and separation from God in the world of their own making. As the story goes, their collective choice to ignore the voice of God and then deny responsibility for that choice when faced with accountability resulted in their expulsion from the Garden of Eden. The initial experience must have been excruciating. The narrative of their irresponsibility seems to imply that they experienced a new sensation: "Then the eyes of both were opened, and they knew that they were naked . . ." (Gen. 3:7). We also see this moment of pain met with God's mercy when just a few verses later the story recalls that ". . . the LORD God made garments of skins for the man and for his wife, and clothed them" (Gen. 3:21). Whereas the initial transgression sowed the seed of alienation, it might be that God's act of mercy planted the seed of hope.

All was not lost. The hope of healing and reconciliation might have been communicated in that seemingly insignificant moment when the Divine Creator became the Divine Tailor.

We see this hope popping up throughout the Scriptures. We see it beneath the horror of Noah and the Great Flood, where God hopes that healing and reconciliation will follow the sheer devastation of the world. We see it again when God promises Abraham and Sarah and their family a home to bless the nations of the world, only to have this hope for a family delayed. We hear this hope in the cries of the Israelites who yearned for God's freedom and hungered for their long-promised homeland. We hear it again when, after centuries of living in this homeland, they were carried away in chains. Underneath the cries, the pain, the anxiety, and the suffering that had echoed across cultures, languages, and geography there lived the hope that God would complete what God started: not only the renewal of the face of the whole earth, but also the raising of humanity to be the children of God capable of taking our rightful place in God's Creation. A healed and reconciled world brings along with it the full human vocation.

This hope is not the sole purchase of Jewish and Christian people. There is something fundamentally human about this hope. People from varying religious and moral traditions, personal and cultural experiences have given voice to the hope that the world can be, indeed will be, a transformed place. Perhaps this is why Dr. King's message resonated so deeply with people in the United States of America and across the globe. Although it was rooted in the Jewish prophetic tradition and interpreted through the life and ministry of Jesus, it spoke to a deep yearning and hunger.

Liturgy as Bread for the Word

Our liturgical tradition is compelling and challenging because it speaks to this nagging human hunger. Furthermore, contrary to popular, muddled, and unclear versions of Christianity, our liturgical practice speaks to the nagging human hunger for healing and reconciliation in light of its purpose: to serve the kingdom of God. The goal of the Church is not personal happiness or self-fulfillment. Such goals continue to make idols of humans rather than pointing us back to our life-giving and life-sustaining connection to our Creator. The purpose of the Church is to point to and serve the kingdom of God, on earth as it is in heaven, a kingdom, a Way of Life marked by reconciliation and healing.

Whenever Jesus speaks about the kingdom of God, he does so by employing the medium of parables. A parable, according to C.H. Dodd, is "a metaphor or simile drawn from nature of common life, arresting the hearer by its vividness or strangeness, and leaving the mind in sufficient doubt about its precise application to tease the mind into active thought" (Dodd, *The Parables of the Kingdom*, 5). Amy-Jill Levine echoes this notion when she says that parables are "a genre that is designed to surprise, challenge, shake up, or indict" (Levine, *Short Stories by Jesus*, 4). Thus, when Jesus employs parables like that of the "Wise and Foolish Bridesmaids" (Matt. 25:1–13), the "Pearl of Great Price" (Matt. 13:45), the "Lost Coin" (Luke 15:8–10), or the "Wedding

Banquet" (Luke 14:7–14), he isn't trying to communicate a clear definition of the kingdom of God; rather, he is attempting to shake up our conventional way of thinking to help us more readily experience and inherit the kingdom.

The parables of Jesus make clear that living in the kingdom of God is living with values different from those that appear to be "normal" in our world. Jesus also communicates this message through poetic parallels, what we hear in his famous Beatitudes, part of this larger Sermon on the Mount:

> Blessed are the poor in spirit, for theirs is the kingdom of heaven.
>> Blessed are those who mourn, for they will be comforted.
>> Blessed are the meek, for they will inherit the earth.
>> Blessed are those who hunger and thirst for righteousness, for they will be filled.
>> Blessed are the merciful, for they will receive mercy.
>> Blessed are the pure in heart, for they will see God.
>> Blessed are the peacemakers, for they will be called children of God.
>> Blessed are those who are persecuted for righteousness' sake, for theirs is the kingdom of heaven.
>> Blessed are you when people revile you and persecute you and utter all kinds of evil against you falsely on my account. Rejoice and be glad, for your reward is great in heaven, for in the same way they persecuted the prophets who were before you.

—Matt. 5:3–12

The kingdom of God, rooted in healing and reconciliation, is one where the conventional ways of the world are turned on their heads. The last are first. The poor are exalted. The meek, not the powerful or well connected, inherit the earth. It would seem that the teaching of Jesus points us back to the difficult work of reconciliation. To serve the kind of world presented in the Gospels, we must practice the inside-out, upside-down values of the kingdom of God. Indeed, this compelling message is what made Christianity so popular initially. It was a faith that spoke to the lingering hope that lives in every human heart by indicting the status quo as both corrupt and feckless. The Christian faith might have also been so popular because however good it was at naming what it stood against, it was better at naming what it stood for. In the expansive and tantalizing language of the kingdom of God, Jesus cast a vision for a whole new world that lives above, below, within, and alongside this world we now inhabit.

Over the centuries, this image of the kingdom of God was domesticated and distorted. Many thought the kingdom of God was a geopolitical reality, comprising the so-called Christian realms of a particular branch of Christianity. Kelly Brown Douglas reminds us that many of the initial founders of the United States thought they were bringing the kingdom of God to earth in their American project (Douglas, *Stand Your Ground*, 25). It does not take a well-trained historian to see that history is littered with the wreckage and human casualties of kingdoms and states that erroneously sought to bring the kingdom of God to the earth by force, by coercion. Rather than serving as a rallying cry for a new, more just, more compassionate, more loving world, the "kingdom of God" became associated with oppression, violence, and exploitation. In many ways, much of the contemporary work of the Church is to dig through the wreckage created by our allegiance to wealth and power and rediscover the upside-down, inside-out values of the kingdom of God. Such work will truly enable us to be reconcilers and healers.

Expanding Our Understanding of the Kingdom of God

The kingdom of God is something far more powerful and challenging than a nation state. The power of the kingdom of God is found in love, in a love that is other-oriented. As we saw in earlier chapters, the love that we talk about here is not the romantic or sentimental notion of love. Frederick Bauerschmidt argues that the divine love we seek is experienced in the heart of the Holy Trinity itself. He writes:

> In the mystery of the Trinity we glimpse the love that God is, the love that is the source of our being . . . The triune God . . . is freed from self-seeking, from rivalry, from objectification, from the torments of passion and obsession . . . The God who is Father, Son, and Spirit is interpersonal life unmarred by rivalry and self-seeking because it is grounded in the eternal act of kindness that is God's essence. This divine kindness is the endless sea of love upon which our created being floats. This is the love that can heal the failures of our human loves.
>
> —Bauerschmidt, *The Love That Is God*, 21

The power of the kingdom of God is found in the strength of the divine love that is at its heart.

It is also important to note how we experience the great power of the kingdom of God. We experience it in stillness, in small moments, in humility, and in the unexpected. We experience it in the words of grace spoken over us, in the flowing of water and the scent of olive oil on the brow, in the sip of fragrant wine and the taste of bread, in the hands placed on our heads as words of forgiveness or healing are uttered. Instead of coming armed and on a horseback, the kingdom, that is, the presence of God comes to us meek and swaddled in a manger. It is a true grassroots movement, where the same hopeful hearts that yearn for the coming of a brighter day also become the fertile ground for the growth of the kingdom. We yearn for a reconciled world, so God freely offers us mercy and forgiveness to make us agents of reconciliation. We yearn for a healed world, so God heals us and makes us healers. Our liturgical practice anticipates both our individual need for healing and reconciliation and that need our world has for people to live out those vocations. Jesus tells us "The harvest is plentiful, but the laborers are few; therefore, ask the Lord of the harvest to send out laborers into his harvest" (Matt. 9:37–38).

The leap between the personal experience of healing and reconciliation to the global or cosmic is challenging. As Americans, we are steeped in a culture of "rugged individualism." So many of our popular myths and stories celebrate the individual at the expense of the community; much of the political rhetoric prizes "individual liberty" at the expense of corporate responsibility. As a result, much of the experience of religion in the United States is held in the realm of the private and individual experience. To be certain, this separation between the individual and the collective is to a certain degree the result of a separation of "church and state," which is implicit in United States political doctrine. The freedom of and from religion is a core principle that sets the United States apart from many other nations.

At the same time, a religious tradition of individualism inhibits our ability to live into the full breadth of our Christian tradition. When the social separation of "church" and "state" causes the division between what Howard Thurman calls the "God of Religion" and the "God of Life," we need to intervene to ensure the integral practice of the Christian faith. (Thurman, *The Growing Edge*, 57). The duality that dominates our practice of faith—personal versus collective, religious versus political—is simply not within the worldview of Christians throughout the majority of our history. This means that the personal and collective are connected just as are the religious and the political. When the Church speaks of the kingdom of God, it is not cordoning off certain parts of our lives. The kingdom of God encompasses all aspects of our lives and so much more. Therefore, to experience healing and reconciliation personally is to connect to the collective hope for healing and reconciliation. We catch a glimpse of the kingdom of God to serve its light in the world.

This means that healing is intended to be a global reality. For the past 150 years, we have witnessed the growing degradation of the earth through human-made pollution and now we are acutely aware of climate change and the devastation it brings, especially to poorer nations and their people. The Psalms teach us that "the earth is the Lord's and all that is in it, the world, and those who live in it" (24:1). The Prayer Book challenges us to recognize the sin of earth's degradation and subsequent ill health: "For our waste and pollution of your creation, and our lack of concern for those who come after us, accept our repentance" (Ash Wednesday "Litany of Penitence"). The prayers ask for God's guidance: "For the good earth which God has given us, and for the wisdom and will to conserve it, let us pray to the Lord" ("The Prayers"). Christian commitment to healing is not only personal or interpersonal; it extends to the earth and its many creatures.

That said, there is also a sense that the healing and reconciliation we practice and experience liturgically is somehow unfinished. Our specific experience with the liturgical rites for Ministration to the Sick and the Reconciliation of a Penitent are open to being repeated. We return to them because the earth, its many creatures, and we ourselves do not yet live in the fullness of the kingdom of God. Christ is truly present with us and for us in the sacraments, but the sacraments themselves do not confine or pin down that presence. Rather, they open us to a wider healing and lead us to the future. We return to them because we continue to seek nourishment, strength, forgiveness, and healing.

As such, our liturgical experience of healing and reconciliation also holds space for grief. We will experience these rites over and over again because while the presence of Christ is constant, our awareness of it, marred by self-interest and easy distraction, has a remarkably short half-life.

Therefore, the liturgical experience of healing and reconciliation opens our vision to the second coming of Christ. He dwells in the future and in our present. Our hope is grounded in his healing and reconciling presence in the present, yet a present grounded in hope, a hope that leads us into the future. Because of his presence now—coming to us from the future—we actually have something compelling to offer the world. Our ability to speak to the longing and hope of humanity is grounded in the work Jesus Christ accomplished and continues to accomplish among us and through us in the present. We can speak because he lives and because his life is but the first fruit of the new life that is coming to the world. All Christian liturgy participates in God's divine liturgy: the healing and reconciliation of the world. Our rituals for healing and reconciliation are no different. They have great importance for us personally, but as we've seen throughout our exploration, they also have global and cosmic ramifications as well.

The human story is fraught with challenge. "In the beginning" humans beings turned away from the love of God by abusing their freedom and choosing instead to put themselves at the center of our lives. Self-interest has not evaporated over the millennia. Ever after the human experience has been one of pain and suffering experienced on every level of the human experience: from the personal to the collective. The relentless human hope for healing and reconciliation has also accompanied this experience and has given meaning to moments in our history when we, like Dr. King, went up to the mountaintop and looked over to see that a new world was not only possible and necessary, but also promised. Still, suffering and pain endure.

To this, the Christian faith offers the fulfillment of our hope: the kingdom of God, a kingdom in which healing, wholeness, mercy, and forgiveness abound. To enter it, we are called to be born from above in baptism, be marked with the cross of Christ, and enter this world as people committed to forgiveness and healing. For many of us, this is the work of a lifetime. Thurman suggests that process is the heart of the religious experience, stating that "There need not be only a single rebirth, but again and again a man may be reborn until at last there is nothing that stands between him and God." (Thurman, *The Creative Encounter*, 40). Each time we enact our healing and reconciliation liturgically, a bit of Creation is born again and brought into closer fellowship with the death and resurrection of Jesus Christ. This, no doubt, is the source of great rejoicing in heaven, because the great and glorious day of our reunion is brought that much closer.

Reflection Questions

1. Scripture uses many images, parables, and stories to describe the kingdom of God. Which ones are most compelling to you and why?

2. Where do you see hope being enacted in our community and world? Who are the bearers of that hope? What vision of the world do these individuals and communities hold up for us?

3. We affirm our belief in the "Second Coming of Jesus" each time we gather as a worshiping community. Why is this affirmation key to the Christian witness in our world today?

Bibliography

Augustine. *The City of God*, translated by Marcus Dods. New York: Random House, 1950.

Augustine. *The Confessions*, translated by Maria Boulding, O.S.B. New York: Vintage Books, 1997.

Bauerschmidt, Frederick Christian. *The Love That Is God: An Invitation to the Christian Faith*. Grand Rapids, MI: William B. Eerdmans Publishing Company, 2020.

Dodd, C.H. *The Parables of the Kingdom*. New York: Charles Scribner's Sons, 1961.

Douglas, Kelly Brown. *Stand Your Ground: Black Bodies and the Justice of God*. Maryknoll, NY: Orbis, 2015.

Gatta, Julia and Martin Smith. *Go in Peace: The Art of Hearing Confessions*. New York: Morehouse Publishing, 2012.

Held, Shai. *The Heart of Torah*, Vol. 1: *Essays on the Weekly Torah Portion: Genesis and Exodus*. Philadelphia: Jewish Publication Society, 2017.

King, Martin Luther, Jr. *A Testament of Hope: the Essential Writings and Speeches of Martin Luther King, Jr.*. Edited by James Washington. New York: HarperCollins, 1991.

Levine, Amy-Jill. *Short Stories by Jesus: The Enigmatic Parables of a Controversial Rabbi*. New York: HarperCollins, 2014.

Lewis, C.S. *The Complete C.S. Lewis Signature Classics*. New York: HarperOne, 2002.

Macquarrie, John. *A Guide to the Sacraments*. London: SCM Press Ltd., 1997.

Mitchell, Lee and Ruth Meyers. *Praying Shapes Believing: A Theological Commentary on the Book of Common Prayer*. New York: Seabury Books, 2016.

Nouwen, Henri. *The Wounded Healer: Ministry in Contemporary Society*. New York: Image Doubleday, 1972.

Talley, Thomas J. *Worship: Reforming Tradition*. Washington, DC: Pastoral Press, 1990.

Thurman, Howard. *The Creative Encounter*. Richmond, IN: Friends United Press, 1954.

Thurman, Howard. *The Growing Edge*. Richmond, IN: Friends United Press, 1956.

Williams, Rowan. *Being Christian: Baptism, Bible, Eucharist, Prayer*. Grand Rapids, MI: William B. Eerdmans Publishing Company, 2014.

Wright, N.T. *Paul: A Biography*. New York: HarperOne, 2018.

Wright, N.T. *The Day the Revolution Began: Reconsidering the Meaning of Jesus's Crucifixion*. New York: HarperOne, 2016.

9 781640 654204